Football School

Name: ....

Class: ....

Coaches: ....

Kickito Ergo Sum

First published 2019 by Walker Books Ltd
87 Vauxhall Walk, London SE11 5HJ

2 4 6 8 10 9 7 5 3 1

Text © 2019 Walker Books Ltd
Illustrations © 2019 Spike Gerrell

The right of Spike Gerrell to be identified as illustrator of this work has been
asserted by him in accordance with the Copyright, Designs and Patents Act 1988

This book has been typeset in Palatino

Printed and bound by CPI Group (UK) Ltd, Croydon CR0 4YY

British Library Cataloguing in Publication Data:
a catalogue record for this book is available from the British Library

ISBN 978-1-4063-9307-1

WALKER
BOOKS

FSC
www.fsc.org
MIX
Paper from
responsible sources
FSC® C020471

www.walker.co.uk
www.footballschool.co

FOOTBALL SCHOOL

THE INCREDIBLE JOKE BOOK

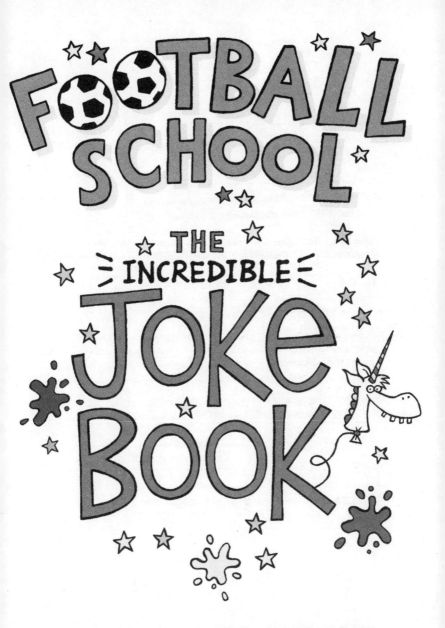

Alex Bellos & Ben Lyttleton
Illustrated by Spike Gerrell

Hi, I'm Alex!
And I'm Ben!
We're your coaches.
Or jokers...
Because this is Football School's Incredible Joke Book!
We will be celebrating the funny side of football.
Join us as we guffaw at goalkeepers and giggle at goals!
Make mischief with midfielders...
And have fun with farcical forwards.
You actually look a bit funny!
Must be because this is a joke book and I'm in a funny mood!
AB
BL

We know that laughter is the best medicine for us all...
Even if you're not injured!
Ouch – that's close to the bone!
We've also included some limericks. Here's one to kick us off.
There once were two authors of Football School,
Who loved laughing and playing the fool,
They wrote this joke book
So people would look
And say, "Wow, football jokes are dead cool!"
At Football School, you become a smarter footballer.
But this book will make you a funnier one!
That's no joke!
Have fun!
AB
BL

CONTENTS

Which dinosaur would you want on your team?

A triceratops – because you'd always get three points.

A terrible striker called Ed,
Who played for a team wearing red,
When he shot from afar
It went over the bar
And knocked out a fan in Row Z!

Did you hear about the smelly footballer?

He was scent off for an early bath.

Doctor, doctor! I think I need an operation. I can't get my socks off.

Try taking your boots off first!

What kind of shot can cut through any defence?

A scissor kick

Did you hear about the winger who stole parts of the pitch?

She kept on taking corners.

Manager: **Just because you're in the England squad, it doesn't mean you can skip morning training, you know!**

Player: But, boss, you told me I'd been picked for the three lie-ins.

Why did the supernatural team get knocked out of the cup?

The ghoulkeeper had a horror show.

What do you call a girl who hangs around the goalposts throughout the match?

Annette

Which player always tidies up the dressing room after his team-mates have left?

The sweeper

Player: **Boss, how come you've picked a baby to play on the wing?**

Manager: Because he's the best dribbler in town.

Why do train drivers make great wing-backs?

They're brilliant at getting up and down the line.

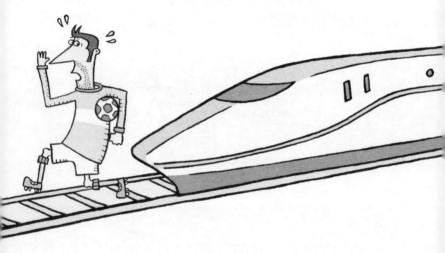

Did you hear about the jeweller who got picked in centre-midfield?

She ran rings around the opposition.

**Why was the
peacock sent off?**

It was a professional fowl.

**Referee: That was a shocking tackle!
I'm sending you off.**

Player: But ref, you said it
was injury time!

Which player never turns up for work?

The striker

What do you call someone who sets up camp at the side of the pitch, lights a fire and starts taking notes?

A scout

Player 1: **Why's Ollie so sad today?**

Player 2: The boss told him that he was going to be left-back.

Player 1: **What's wrong with that?**

Player 2: He meant left-back on the team bus!

Why was the midfielder brilliant at fishing?

Because she had a great tackle.

Manager: You idiots! Why are you wearing swimshorts and sunglasses?

Team: But, boss, you told us to bring our away kit.

I once knew a winger called Pete,
Who learned all his tricks in the street.
He tried a stepover
And promptly fell over
Since the ball got caught up in his feet!

Did you hear about the footballer who couldn't swim?

They gave him the captain's armband.

Did you hear about the player who could swim underwater?

She was a supersub.

Did you hear about the striker who didn't wash his face before bed?

He got penalty spots.

Captain: **Why are you wearing fake ears and a bushy tail?**

Striker: The boss said she wanted me to play like a fox in the box!

What style of football do cows play?

Pass and moo-ve

Player:	**Hey, boss, how come there's a duck costume on my peg in the changing room?**
Manager:	You're rubbish at football, so we've made you the mascot.

What do you call a rugby player on a football pitch?

Lost

Player 1: **How come the new coach carries a broom and a massive set of keys everywhere he goes?**

Player 2: He's only a caretaker manager!

What type of football do bees love?

Hive-a-side

Doctor, doctor! I feel so tired after matches. Can you give me anything?

I can give you some advice – it's time you retired.

I knew a young keeper, Yvette,
Who ended up really upset.
In her very first match,
When she jumped for a catch,
She palmed the ball into the net!

Manager: After your performance this season, I'm giving you something extra this summer.

Player: Thanks, boss, what is it?

Manager: A transfer. You're useless!

Why did the referee tell the fourth official to run up the touchline?

The linesman was flagging.

Referee: **Come here, sonny. You're getting a yellow card for that terrible dive.**

Player: Aww ... be fair, ref, I can't swim!

Why did Gareth Bale get thrown off the plane?

He kept running up the wings.

How does Cristiano Ronaldo get into his house?

Through the Ballon D'Or

Did you hear about the team who signed a USA World Cup star?

They Rose to a new Lavelle.

What's a chip-shop owner's favourite football show?

Catch of the Day, with Gary Vinegar

Why does Jadon Sancho's dad think he's too cheeky?

Well, he is a little forward.

Who is a farmer's favourite pundit?

Alan Shearer

Why did one of the world's best players keep getting told off by his mum?

Because he was Messi!

Why did Emma Hayes teach her squad DIY?

She wanted her team to hammer the opposition.

**Why did Paul Pogba
cry on his birthday?**

He only got red cards.

**What do you call a forward
who loves lettuce?**

Mo Salad

What do the world's best players have as a pre-match meal?

Ada Hegerberger and chips

Fan 1: **Did you know that Mauricio Pochettino is a massive Lego fan?**

Fan 2: Yeah, he can build a great team.

Fan 1: **Who's that coach arriving at the stadium on a horse?**

Fan 2: That's Jürgen Klippety-Klopp!

Which defender always finishes third in races?

Lucy Bronze

Who is the Bank of England's favourite player?

Raheem Sterling

The super striker Ellen White,
At parties on Halloween night,
Doesn't need to dress up
Or wear scary make-up,
She already gives goalies a fright!

Which goalkeeper works on a farm?

Jordan Pitchfork

- 38 -

Why is it always windy when England play at Wembley?

Because there's a Harry Kane!

Which player can run across the pitch the fastest?

Megan Rapido

Why did Everton sell their striker?

He couldn't shoot for Toffees.

Which team do ghosts support?

Frighten & Hove Albion

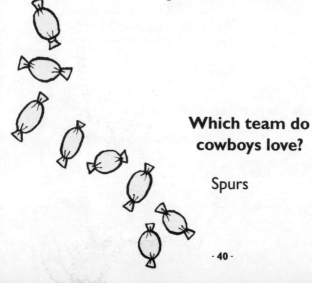

Which team do cowboys love?

Spurs

What's an ice-cream lover's favourite team?

Aston Vanilla

Which team always start a match with a bang?

The Gunners

Which Spanish side is certain to get relegated?

Pathetico Madrid

What's a Spanish postman's favourite team?

Parcel-owner

There was a team called United,
Whose fans would get over-excited.
Their stars were too old
So of course they got sold
And the fans were left rather divided!

Why are Southampton the Pope's favourite team?

Because all the players are Saints!

Which team does all their training in national parks?

Rangers

Why are Crystal Palace guaranteed to fly up the table?

Because they're the Eagles!

Which books do Stoke City fans love?

THE HARRY POTTERS

Which Italian team give all their players dictionaries?

ABC Milan

The Championship team were called City.
Their football was all very pretty,
Till the day they slipped up,
Got knocked out of the Cup,
'Cause it turned out they weren't very gritty!

What's a football fan's favourite sandwich?

West Ham and Mustard

Which team did Robin Hood support?

Nottingham Forest

What are sticky, full of fruit and play at Stamford Bridge?

Chelsea buns

FOOTBALL RULES THE WORLD

What's a goal-scorer's favourite drink?

Penal-tea

Did you hear about the Jedi football match?

It finished Obi-Wan Kenobi-Nil.

What's the most popular film in Brazil?

Finding Neymar

Where can you watch dragons, elves and goblins play against each other?

In the Fantasy Football League

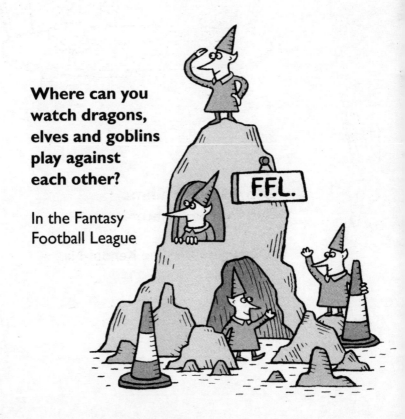

Why did the referee get a job at the theatre?

She was great at booking people.

Did you hear the scores in The Three Musketeers' matches?

One was four–all and the rest were all four–one.

Why did the footballer wear her boots on her ears?

She loved sole music.

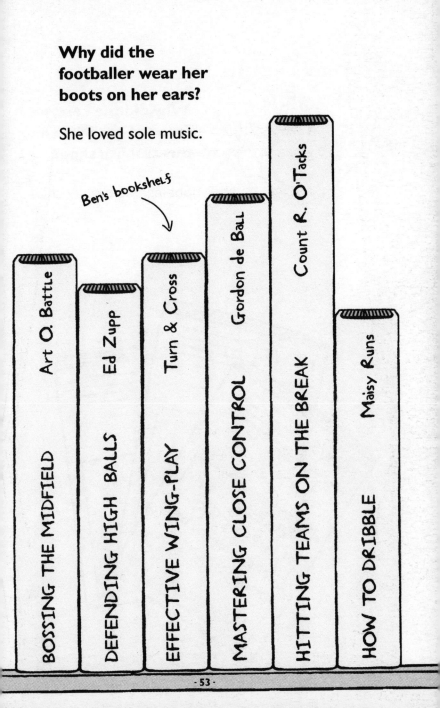

Ben's bookshelf

Art O. Battle — BOSSING THE MIDFIELD

Ed Zupp — DEFENDING HIGH BALLS

Turn & Cross — EFFECTIVE WING-PLAY

Gordon de Ball — MASTERING CLOSE CONTROL

Count R. O'Tacks — HITTING TEAMS ON THE BREAK

Maisy Runs — HOW TO DRIBBLE

Why did the centre-forward get thrown out of a fish shop?

She tried a cheeky chip.

What do Leicester City fans read in the morning?

Bluespapers

Why can't you play football in the desert?

There are too many cheetahs!

How do strikers like their eggs at breakfast time?

Goal-poached

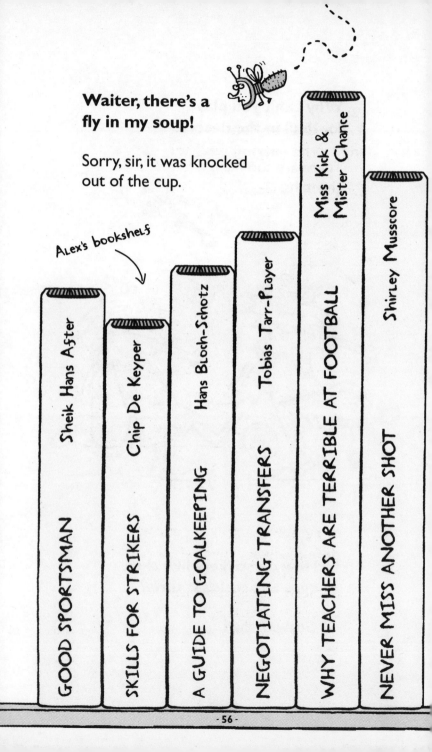

What did the centre-forward say to the singing winger?

On me 'Ed, Sheeran!

Why are teachers great at defending set pieces?

Because they get so much practice at marking!

Why do footballers take up rugby at Easter?

So they can use egg-shaped balls

Which fixture is played every Halloween?

Norwitch City v. Werewolverhampton Wanderers

Where do footballers spend their holidays?

Training camps

Why did the footballer get banned from playing on his birthday?

Because he got so many cards!

FUNNY FAN ZONE

Why do Liverpool fans love dogs?

Because they'll *Never Walk Alone!*

Where do fans like to go dancing?

At a Foot Ball

Did you hear about the soldier football fans who went to a match?

They invaded the pitch.

Fan 1: **Why are you wearing those ridiculous trousers?**

Fan 2: My dad told me flares added to the match atmosphere.

Knock, knock!
Who's there?
Casey
Casey who?
**"Casey Ra-Sera,
Whatever will be will be,
We're going to Wem-ber-ley!"**

**What do hard-core Italian
fans do to keep fit?**

They run ultra-marathons.

**Why did the red-hot fan
have to miss the match?**

She had football fever.

In the crowd a spectator called Mitch,
Suffered an unexpected itch.
He squirmed in his seat
And wriggled his feet
Till he tumbled right onto the pitch!

What's black and white and red all over?

A Newcastle fan who's really angry about the result!

Why can't Shrewsbury Town fans buy tea or coffee at matches?

Because they've got no cups!

A diehard fan called Jo-May,
Sees her team play home and away.
With a bit more luck
They might not suck
And she could see them win big one day!

Knock, knock!

Sorry, sir, I'm not letting you in without a ticket.

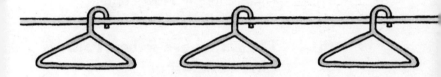

Where do American fans buy their replica kits?

New Jersey

Fan 1: Do you know, I've had a season ticket for 30 years and I've never seen my team lose!

Fan 2: That's amazing. How come?

Fan 1: The games are so bad, I always leave at half-time!

Knock, knock!
Who's there?
Ivor
Ivor who?
Ivor Sore Throat from all that chanting!

**What do gorillas love
to see players try?**

Banana shots

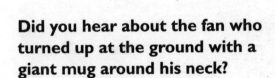

**Did you hear about the fan who
turned up at the ground with a
giant mug around his neck?**

It was a big cup tie.

There was a supporter called Phil,
A fan of a team with no skill.
Each week he would go
But always feel low
Since they lost all their matches five-nil!

**What type of music do
Birmingham City fans love?**

The Blues

Which team does the Queen support?

Chelsea, because they play in royal blue!

Fan 1: **My team's like a teabag.**

Fan 2: What do you mean?

Fan 1: **They never stay in the cup for long!**

Why are monks great football fans?

They get so much practice at chanting.

Knock, knock!
Who's there?
Cam
Cam who?
"Cam On You Blu-ues!"

What do football fans love on TV?

Matchday programmes

Why do artists go to matches in groups?

So they'll never chalk alone!

Why do snowmen love going to football games?

They can wear their scarves and bobble hats.

Why did the fan take an armchair and a TV to the stadium?

It was a home game.

What do babies take to games?

Rattles

Knock, knock!
Who's there?
Owen
Owen who?
**"Owen the Spurs
go marchin' in…"**

MATCH DAY MAYHEM

Where would you go to watch a team full of pensioners?

Granfield

Knock, knock!
Who's there?
Doug
Doug who?
Doug Out

What do you call a stadium at the North Pole?

Cold Trafford

Where's the best place to watch night matches?

The Stadium of Light

Which bit of the pitch smells of perfume?

The scenter circle

Why did the penalty area go to the gym?

To see the six yard box!

What did the scouts do when they had no football pitch?

They looked for a Nou Camp.

Why did the groundsman appear on *X Factor*?

He was pitch perfect.

How do players leave their clubs?

Through the transfer window

What's the grumpiest thing on a football pitch?

The crossbar

Why are stadiums like railways?

They both have tunnels.

Why are football grounds always so cool?

Because of all the fans!

Where do spiders play Cup Finals?

Webley

Knock, knock!
Who's there?
Dan
Dan who?
Dan't go through that turnstile, that's the away end!

Why did the chicken cross the road?

Because the stadium was on the other side!

Did you hear what happened when the footballer went for a kickabout in the park?

She was left on the bench.

How can you tell if a pitch is waterlogged?

Turn on the floodlights!

Where do the ghosts of Manchester United players end up?

The Theatre of Screams

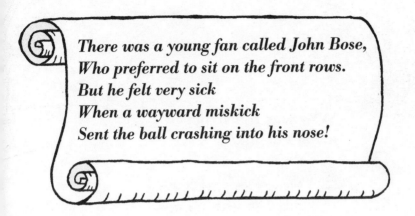

There was a young fan called John Bose,
Who preferred to sit on the front rows.
But he felt very sick
When a wayward miskick
Sent the ball crashing into his nose!

Did you hear about the player
who fell in love with the pitch?

He kept hugging the touchline.

Why was the striker always drunk?

He kept hitting the bar.

Did you hear about the world's worst referee?

He called for VAR to decide who'd won the toss.

The young football fan, Kevin Kites,
Did not have a good head for heights.
When he sat in the stands
He put his head in his hands
As the view gave him terrible frights!

Where do managers do their DIY?

In the technical area

Fan 1: How do you spot the opposition's best player during the warm-up?

Fan 2: She's the one doing star jumps.

Did you hear about the stadium that got really upset when its team got relegated?

It ended up in tiers.

Policeman:	**I'm sorry, sir. You can't take that bow and arrow into the stadium.**
Fan:	But, officer ... I'm only an autograph hunter!

SILLY SAYINGS AND CLUELESS COMMENTARY

Player I: **What's the boss doing? I heard he just signed a magician.**

Player 2: Yes, but they reckon he's got a wand for a left foot.

Why do the best strikers have big noses?

So they can sniff out opportunities

Did you hear about the match played on a hexagonal pitch?

It was a real six-pointer.

Why are goalkeepers brilliant at geometry?

They always get their angles right.

Doctor, doctor! What can I take to stop my team losing?

Take each game as it comes.

Why do maths teachers love football?

It's a game of two halves.

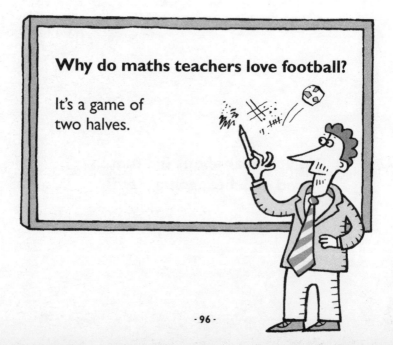

How did the astronaut feel after her team won the cup?

Over the moon

Manager: **Look at the state of this pitch. There are lumps all over it!**

Groundsman: Don't worry, boss. These things even themselves out over the course of a season.

Referee: **Look, will you stop playing. I blew the final whistle five minutes ago!**

Player: But, ref, the manager told us to give 110%!

Why did the youth team have to dig up the pitch?

Because they had talent in spades!

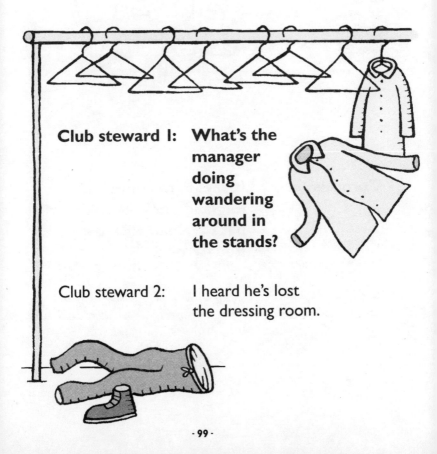

Club steward 1: **What's the manager doing wandering around in the stands?**

Club steward 2: I heard he's lost the dressing room.

Did you hear about the writers who've formed a football team?

It's a great team on paper.

Commentator: **It says in my notes that England's new centre-back trained with the Red Arrows.**

Pundit: Well, she is great in the air!

Why did the team walk into the dressing room naked?

They left everything on the pitch.

Commentator: **The goalkeeper has just pulled a rabbit out of his glovebag!**

Pundit: It's just the magic of the FA Cup, isn't it?

Why did the manager call in a plumber?

To sort out his leaky defence

Interviewer:	Your new striker certainly knows where the goal is!
Manager:	Well, I'd be worried if she didn't.

The striker sat on the touchline reading instructions for half an hour, then strolled onto the pitch and belted the ball into the top corner.

It was a textbook finish!

Knock, knock!
Who's there?
Mark
Mark who?
Mark de Mann

Why did the manager bring a double-decker to training?

She wanted her defenders to park the bus.

Did you hear about the club Christmas party where no one ate the buffet?

The manager told his captain it was time he stepped up to the plate.

Which player brings a rope to training?

The skipper

Commentator: **This player spends every morning training and every afternoon in the library.**

Pundit: He reads the game very well!

What lights up a football stadium?

A match

Why don't players like scoring at their home ground?

Because away goals rule!

Manager: Cinderella, stop giving them so much space! You shall go to the ball!

Why did everyone hate playing the team of actors?

They were always showboating.

Did you hear about the player who ate sweetcorn before every match?

She was famous for her maize-y runs.

FINAL WHISTLE

Did you hear about the manager who was always taking the squad on trips?

He made a great coach.

What do track and field athletes do when they fancy a kickabout?

Use long jumpers for goalposts

**Why couldn't the
car play football?**

It only had one boot.

**What did the striker get
at the dentist?**

A brace

What do you call a Scottish goal-scorer?

Mac O' the Net

Why do central defenders do well at school?

They really know how to use their heads.

What's a striker's favourite magic routine?

A hat trick

Did you hear what happened when the coach turned up at a school sports day?

She won the sack race.

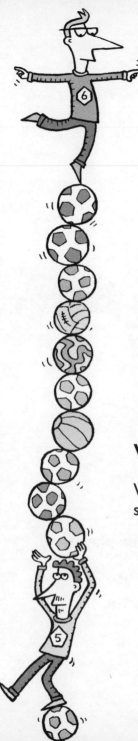

Did you hear about the cricketer who signed for her local football team?

She was a great all-rounder.

When is a football not round?

When it's a square ball

Why do fish make rubbish goalkeepers?

They don't like playing in nets.

Did you hear about the player who loved wildlife?

He got stuck in the reserves.

**Why did the chicken cross
the halfway line?**

It was changing ends for the
second half.

**Did you hear about the dog that
became a professional footballer?**

It was brilliant at keepy-puppies.

What do wingers do when they need the toilet?

Cross their legs
instead of
the ball

Interviewer: **Would you ever resort to playing the long ball?**

Manager: No, we'll always use a round one.

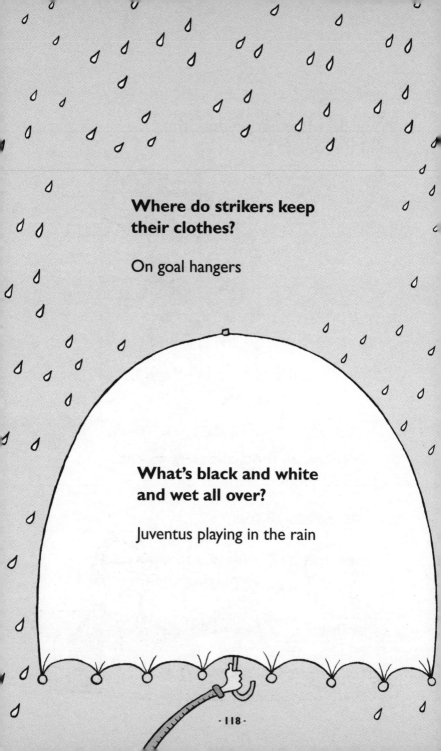

Where do strikers keep their clothes?

On goal hangers

What's black and white and wet all over?

Juventus playing in the rain

How can you tell that referees are always happy?

You can hear them whistle while they work.

Where do footballers sit to eat their dinner?

At the League Table

What's an insect's favourite European league?

Serie Bee

What cup do Spanish fishermen play for?

The Copa del Stingray

What kind of competition do birdwatchers most enjoy?

Round-robin tournaments

Who organises matches between giants?

FI-FA Fo Fum

Why did the centipede's dad stop him playing football?

He couldn't afford to buy him new boots.

How did the pig get injured?

He pulled a hamstring.

What kind of ship is guaranteed never to go down?

A Premiership

What happens to managers who do a really good job?

They get promoted.

We've reached the end of the book!
Oh dear, that's no laughing matter.
It's been great to share some chuckles about the game. We've hooted with laughter, honked with pleasure, tittered, sniggered and split our sides.
The gags about pitches really had me in stitches!
We've met some new players, like Mo Salad, Jordan Pitchfork and Ada Hegerberger!
And some new teams, like Aston Vanilla, Frighten & Hove Albion and Pathetico Madrid!
And even visited new stadiums like Granfield and Cold Trafford!
Brrrrrr!
AB
BL

One last joke for you: what did the goalkeeper say to the football?
Catch you later!
Exactly!
And before we go, we also have one last limerick to share with you!
So the end of this book is quite near,
But there's something we want you to hear,
There's no need to be sad,
The news isn't all bad,
Football School has more books out next year!
See you then!
Ha, ha!
AB
BL

MORE FROM
FOOTBALL SCHOOL

At Football School EVERY lesson is
about football. The series is packed with
awesome true stories, real science and
fascinating facts. You'll find the answers
to these questions and many more:

When do footballers poo?

Why are footballs NOT round?

Who stole the World Cup?

How do you play football on Mars?

**Why are footballers similar
to llamas?**

"We love this book series!"
Match of the Day Weekly

"Hilarious ... packed with amazing football
facts, cartoons, jokes..."
The Week Junior

"Intelligent, inspiring, funny..."
Head of Education, Premier League

NEW SEASON OUT NOW

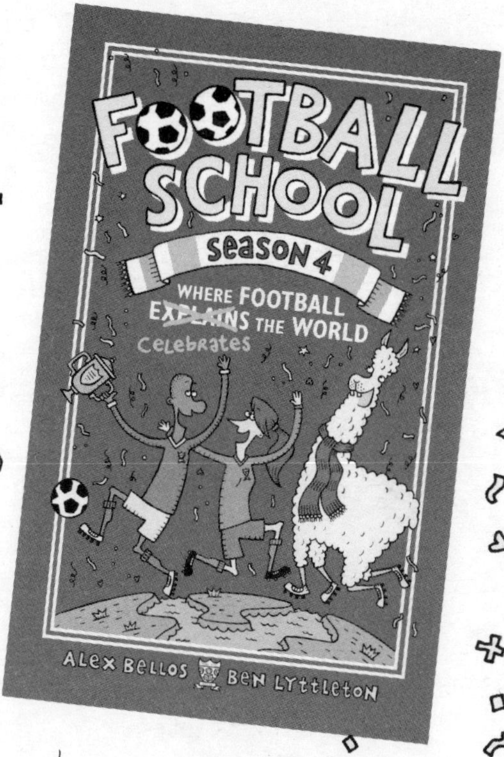

COLLECT THE FOOTBALL SCHOOL SERIES